contents

soups & starters	2
chicken	17
lamb	33
vegetables & salads	47
glossary	62
conversion charts	63
index	64

lentil, bulgar wheat & spinach soup

2 litres water
1 cup (200g) brown lentils
1 cup (160g) bulgar wheat
¼ cup (60ml) olive oil
2 medium white onions (300g), chopped finely
2 cloves garlic, crushed
350g spinach, shredded finely
2 tablespoons coarsely chopped fresh flat-leaf parsley

1 Bring the water to a boil in large saucepan; cook lentils, uncovered, until just tender. Add bulgar wheat, cover; simmer mixture 1 hour, stirring occasionally.
2 Meanwhile, heat oil in medium frying pan; cook onion and garlic, stirring, until browned lightly. Add spinach, cover; remove from heat.
3 Just before serving, add spinach and onion mixture; stir over low heat until heated through.
4 Serve sprinkled with parsley and, if desired, topped with some plain yogurt.

serves 4

chicken & rice soup

1kg chicken thigh fillets, chopped coarsely
4 trimmed sticks celery (300g), chopped finely
1 large onion (200g), chopped finely
2 cloves garlic, crushed
1 cinnamon stick
1 teaspoon cracked black pepper
2 litres (8 cups) water
½ cup (125ml) lemon juice
1 cup (200g) calrose rice (or another short grain rice)
½ cup firmly packed, coarsely chopped flat-leaf parsley
2 tablespoons small fresh mint leaves

1 Combine chicken, celery, onion, garlic, cinnamon, pepper and the water in large saucepan; bring to a boil. Reduce heat to a simmer; cook, covered, 1 hour, skimming surface occasionally.
2 Add juice and rice to soup; simmer, uncovered, stirring occasionally, until rice is tender, stir in parsley.
3 Serve soup topped with mint.

serves 4

meatball soup with crispy pitta

500g minced lamb
1 teaspoon ground allspice
½ teaspoon ground nutmeg
½ cup (125ml) olive oil
1.25 litres (5 cups) chicken stock
¼ cup (50g) white long-grain rice
½ cup (125ml) hot water
1 tablespoon tomato paste
¼ cup firmly packed, finely chopped fresh flat-leaf parsley
crispy pitta
1 large pitta bread
¼ teaspoon cayenne pepper

1 Combine lamb and spices in medium bowl; using hands, knead until meat mixture forms a smooth paste. Shape level teaspoons of meat mixture into balls.
2 Heat oil in large frying pan; cook meatballs, in batches, until just browned.
3 Place stock in large saucepan, bring to a boil; stir in rice and the combined hot water and tomato paste. Reduce heat, add meatballs; simmer soup, uncovered, about 30 minutes or until meatballs are cooked through. Just before serving, stir in parsley.
4 Serve topped with crispy pitta.

crispy pitta Split pitta in half; sprinkle split side with cayenne pepper. Place both rounds, split-side up, on baking trays. Bake in moderately hot oven about 10 minutes or until crisp, cool slightly before breaking into small pieces.

serves 4

kibbi

1 cup (160g) bulgar wheat
600g minced lamb
1 medium onion (150g), grated
1 teaspoon ground allspice
1 teaspoon ground oregano
1 tablespoon olive oil
1 tablespoon water
vegetable oil for shallow-frying
filling
2 teaspoons olive oil
1 small onion (80g), finely chopped
1 tablespoon pine nuts
1 tablespoon slivered almonds
100g minced lamb
½ teaspoon ground allspice
½ teaspoon ground oregano
1 tablespoon chopped fresh mint

1 Place bulgar wheat in bowl, cover with cold water, stand 15 minutes. Drain bulgar wheat, rinse under cold water, drain; squeeze to remove excess moisture.
2 Combine bulgar wheat with lamb, onion, allspice, oregano, olive oil and water in bowl; mix well.
3 Shape ¼ cups of lamb mixture into balls, using damp hands. Hollow out centres of meatballs, using your thumb. Place rounded teaspoons of filling into hollowed centres of meatballs. Shape meatballs into ovals, using damp hands.
4 Shallow-fry kibbi in hot oil in batches until browned all over and cooked through; drain on absorbent paper.

filling Heat oil in pan, add onion, cook, stirring, until onion is soft. Add nuts, cook, stirring, until lightly browned. Add lamb, allspice and oregano, cook, stirring, until lamb is browned. Stir in mint.

makes about 16

lamb kofta

750g minced lamb
1 large onion (200g), finely chopped
2 cloves garlic, crushed
¼ teaspoon ground cloves
¼ teaspoon ground nutmeg
¼ teaspoon ground hot paprika
½ teaspoon ground cumin
½ teaspoon ground coriander
1 teaspoon finely grated lemon rind
¼ cup (40g) pine nuts, finely chopped
½ cup finely chopped fresh parsley

1 Combine lamb, onion, garlic, spices and rind in bowl; mix well.
2 Add nuts and parsley, mix well; cover, refrigerate 30 minutes.
3 Roll tablespoons of mixture into ovals. Thread three ovals onto each skewer.
4 Cook kofta in greased heated griddle pan (or grill or barbecue) in batches until browned and cooked through.

makes about 14
tip Soak bamboo skewers in water for several hours or overnight to prevent them from burning.

lavash bread

1 teaspoon dried yeast
1 teaspoon honey
1 teaspoon sugar
½ cup (125ml) warm water
1¼ cups (185g) plain flour
2 teaspoons salt
¼ teaspoon ground hot paprika
¼ teaspoon cayenne pepper
1 egg white, lightly beaten
2 tablespoons assorted seeds (see tip)

1 Combine yeast with honey and sugar in small bowl, stir in water, cover, stand in warm place about 15 minutes or until mixture is frothy.
2 Sift dry ingredients into large bowl. Stir in yeast mixture, mix to a firm dough. Knead dough on floured surface about 2 minutes or until dough is smooth. Place dough in oiled bowl, cover; refrigerate 45 minutes.
3 Turn dough onto floured surface, knead until smooth. Divide dough in half, roll each half into a 13cm x 60cm rectangle.
4 Prick rectangles with fork, brush lightly with egg white. Cut each rectangle into 16 triangles, sprinkle with seeds. Place triangles about 2cm apart on lightly floured baking trays. Bake in moderate oven about 10 minutes or until browned.
5 Serve with hummus dip, if desired.

makes 32
tips Poppy, caraway and sesame seeds can be used in this recipe. Sometimes this dough will become too elastic and difficult to roll; in this case, cover the dough, stand for 30 minutes then continue as directed.

marinated olives

300g drained black olives
300g drained green olives
2 cloves garlic, sliced thinly
2 lemon wedges
2 sprigs fresh dill
1 tablespoon lemon juice
2 cups (500ml) olive oil

1 Combine olives, garlic, lemon, dill and juice in 1-litre (4-cup) sterilised jar; pour oil over olives, seal jar.

makes 4 cups

cucumber with minted yogurt

2 cucumbers (520g)
2 cups (500ml) plain yogurt
¼ cup finely chopped fresh mint leaves
1 clove garlic, crushed
½ teaspoon ground cumin
1 tablespoon lemon juice

1 Halve cucumbers lengthways, scoop out seeds. Finely chop cucumbers.
2 Combine cucumber with remaining ingredients in medium bowl, cover; refrigerate at least 1 hour before serving.

serves 4

roast chicken with rice stuffing

2 tablespoons plain yogurt
2 tablespoons honey
2 teaspoons olive oil
1.5kg whole chicken
stuffing
2 teaspoons olive oil
1 small onion (80g), chopped finely
½ cup (100g) white calrose rice (or another short grain rice)
1 cup (250ml) chicken stock
2 tablespoons slivered almonds, toasted
2 tablespoons raisins, chopped finely
2 tablespoons finely chopped fresh flat-leaf parsley

1 Whisk yogurt, honey and oil in small bowl until combined.
2 Wash chicken under cold water; pat dry with absorbent paper. Tuck wings under chicken; fill cavity with stuffing, secure with toothpicks, tie legs together with kitchen string. Place chicken on oiled wire rack over baking dish, brush chicken with some of the yogurt mixture; bake, uncovered, in moderate oven 30 minutes.
3 Brush chicken with yogurt mixture, cover with foil; bake 1 hour, brushing chicken with yogurt mixture once more during cooking. Remove foil towards end of cooking time to allow chicken skin to brown.

stuffing Heat oil in small heavy-base saucepan; cook onion, stirring, until browned lightly. Add rice; stir until rice is coated in onion mixture. Stir in stock, bring to boil; simmer, covered, 12 minutes. Remove from heat; stand, covered, 10 minutes. Stir in remaining ingredients.

serves 4

chicken with figs

8 chicken thighs
2 tablespoons plain flour
1½ tablespoons ground coriander
pinch cayenne pepper
1½ teaspoons ground cumin
⅓ cup (80ml) olive oil
2 medium onions, sliced
6 cloves garlic
2 bay leaves
8 fresh figs
1¼ cups (310ml) dry red wine
1 teaspoon chicken stock powder
2 teaspoons grated lemon rind
1 teaspoon lemon juice
2 teaspoons cornflour
1 tablespoon water
2 tablespoons chopped fresh flat-leaf parsley

1 Preheat oven to moderate.
2 Remove skin from chicken. Toss chicken in combined flour and spices, shake away excess flour. Heat oil in frying pan, add chicken in batches, cook until well browned all over; drain on absorbent paper. Add onions and garlic to same pan; cook, covered, over low heat, stirring occasionally, 10 minutes or until onions are very soft.
3 Transfer chicken and onion mixture to large heatproof dish (1.75 litre/7 cup capacity). Add bay leaves, figs and combined wine and stock powder; cook, covered, in moderate oven 1¼ hours or until chicken is very tender.
4 Remove chicken, figs and bay leaves from dish; discard bay leaves. Add rind, juice and blended cornflour and water; stir over heat until mixture boils and thickens.
5 Return chicken and figs to pan, stir until heated through; sprinkle with parsley.

serves 4

barbecued chicken with lemon & garlic

1.5kg chicken pieces on the bone
2 teaspoons ground allspice
1 teaspoon salt
2 teaspoons cracked black pepper
6 cloves garlic, crushed
1 teaspoon finely grated lemon rind
1 tablespoon finely chopped fresh mint leaves
½ cup (125ml) olive oil
½ cup (125ml) lemon juice

1 Make two deep cuts in thickest part of each chicken piece.
2 Combine remaining ingredients in large shallow dish; add chicken, mix well. Cover; refrigerate 3 hours or overnight.
3 Drain chicken over medium bowl; reserve marinade. Barbecue (or grill or char-grill) chicken until browned all over and cooked through completely, brushing occasionally with reserved marinade during cooking.

serves 4

chicken with apricots & cracked wheat

1⅓ cups (200g) dried apricots
¾ cup (180ml) dry white wine
2kg chicken pieces
plain flour
⅓ cup (80ml) olive oil
2 large onions, sliced
2 cloves garlic, crushed
1 tablespoon plain flour, extra
2 bay leaves
3 trimmed celery stalks, chopped
2½ cups (625ml) chicken stock
2 teaspoons honey
2 teaspoons chopped fresh thyme
2 teaspoons chopped fresh
  rosemary
2 teaspoons coriander seeds,
  crushed
1 tablespoon brown vinegar
2 teaspoons chopped fresh thyme,
  extra
2 teaspoons chopped fresh
  rosemary, extra
cracked wheat
2 tablespoons olive oil
2 cups (500ml) water
1 cup (160g) cracked wheat
½ cup (80g) black olives, sliced
2 tablespoons chopped fresh
  parsley

1 Combine apricots and wine in bowl; cover, stand 1 hour.
2 Preheat oven to moderately hot.
3 Toss chicken in flour, shake away excess flour. Heat oil in frying pan; cook chicken, in batches, until browned all over. Transfer chicken to ovenproof dish (3 litre/12 cup capacity). Add onions and garlic to same frying pan; cook, stirring, until onions are soft. Stir in extra flour, cook until grainy.
4 Gradually stir in bay leaves, celery, stock, undrained apricots, honey, thyme, rosemary, seeds and vinegar. Bring to boil; pour mixture over chicken, stir well.
5 Bake, covered, in moderately hot oven 2 hours or until chicken is tender.
6 Meanwhile, make cracked wheat.
7 Stir extra thyme and extra rosemary into chicken; season with salt and pepper to taste.
8 Serve chicken with cracked wheat.

cracked wheat Combine oil and water in saucepan, bring to boil, add wheat; simmer, covered, over low heat 15 minutes. Remove from heat, stand, covered, 10 minutes. Add olives and parsley; season with salt and pepper to taste, stir lightly with fork.

serves 6

chicken kebabs
with garlic sauce

1kg chicken thigh fillets
4 cloves garlic, crushed
1 cup (250ml) lemon juice
¼ cup (60ml) olive oil
1 teaspoon sea salt
garlic sauce
1 bulb garlic (70g approximately), peeled, chopped coarsely
1 egg yolk
2 teaspoons water
2 tablespoons lemon juice
1 cup (250ml) olive oil

1 Cut chicken in 3cm pieces; place in large bowl with combined garlic, juice, oil and salt. Cover tightly; refrigerate 3 hours or overnight, turning occasionally
2 Drain chicken; discard marinade. Thread pieces of chicken on long metal skewers; cook on preheated grill plate (or grill or barbecue) until browned all over and cooked through.
3 Serve with garlic sauce and, if desired, warmed pitta bread.

garlic sauce Blend or process garlic, egg yolk, the water and juice until combined. With motor operating, gradually pour in oil; process until thick

serves 4
makes 360ml garlic sauce

chicken tagine with dates & honey

9 chicken thigh fillets (1kg)
2 tablespoons olive oil
2 medium onions (300g), finely sliced
4 cloves garlic, crushed
1 teaspoon cumin seeds
1 teaspoon ground coriander
1 teaspoon ground ginger
1 teaspoon ground turmeric
1 teaspoon ground cinnamon
½ teaspoon chilli powder
¼ teaspoon ground nutmeg
1½ cups (375ml) chicken stock
1 cup (250ml) water
½ cup (85g) stoned dates, halved
¼ cup (60ml) honey
½ cup (80g) blanched almonds, toasted
1 tablespoon chopped fresh coriander leaves

1 Cut chicken into 3cm strips. Heat 1 tablespoon of the oil in pan, add chicken in batches, cook, stirring, until browned; drain on absorbent paper.
2 Heat remaining oil in same pan, add onions, garlic and spices, cook, stirring, until onions are soft.
3 Return chicken to pan with stock and water, simmer, covered, 1 hour. Remove lid, simmer about 30 minutes or until mixture is thickened slightly and chicken is tender.
4 Stir in dates, honey and nuts; sprinkle with fresh coriander.

serves 4 to 6

braised chicken in tomato sauce

2 tablespoons olive oil
8 chicken thigh fillets (880g), sliced
1 large onion (200g), chopped
2 cloves garlic, finely sliced
1 teaspoon ground coriander
½ teaspoon ground turmeric
¼ teaspoon cayenne pepper
4 medium tomatoes (520g), peeled, chopped
3 cups (750ml) chicken stock
1 cinnamon stick
1 medium green pepper (200g), sliced
200g baby yellow squash, quartered
2 small aubergines (120g), thickly sliced
½ cup (85g) raisins
¼ cup (40g) blanched almonds, toasted
2 tablespoons chopped fresh coriander leaves
couscous
1¾ cups (430ml) water
20g butter, chopped
2 cups (400g) couscous

1 Heat oil in pan, add chicken in batches, cook until browned all over; remove from pan.
2 Add onion and garlic to same pan, cook, stirring, until onion is soft. Add ground spices, cook, stirring, until fragrant. Stir in tomatoes and stock.
3 Return chicken to pan with cinnamon stick, simmer, uncovered, about 30 minutes or until sauce has thickened slightly and chicken is tender, stirring occasionally. Add pepper, squash and aubergines, simmer, uncovered, about 5 minutes or until vegetables are tender. Discard cinnamon stick.
4 Serve chicken mixture on couscous, top with raisins, nuts and fresh coriander.

couscous Bring water to boil in medium pan, stir in butter and couscous; remove from heat, cover, stand about 5 minutes or until water is absorbed.

serves 6

chicken pilaf with apricots

60g ghee
1kg chicken thigh fillets, chopped
2 medium onions (300g), sliced
1 clove garlic, crushed
1 teaspoon ground cumin
1 teaspoon ground coriander
½ teaspoon ground turmeric
½ cup (75g) dried apricots, sliced
2 cups (400g) basmati rice
1 litre (4 cups) chicken stock
¼ cup (35g) currants
½ cup (60g) frozen peas
½ cup (80g) pine nuts, toasted

1 Heat half the ghee in large pan, add chicken in batches, cook until lightly browned all over and tender; drain.
2 Heat remaining ghee in same pan, add onions, garlic and spices, cook, stirring, until onions are soft.
3 Add apricots and rice, stir over heat until rice is coated in spice mixture. Stir in stock, simmer, covered with tight-fitting lid, 15 minutes.
4 Remove from heat, stir in chicken, stand, covered, 15 minutes. Stir in currants, peas and nuts. Top with coriander, if desired.

serves 6

garlic & lemon lamb kebabs

1.5kg lamb leg steaks
3 medium lemons
1 cup (250ml) lemon juice
8 cloves garlic, crushed
¼ cup chopped fresh rosemary
1 tablespoon seasoned pepper
2 tablespoons mild mustard
½ cup (125ml) olive oil
2 tablespoons olive oil, extra
30g butter

1 Cut lamb into 3cm pieces. Using vegetable peeler, peel rind thinly from lemons; cut rind into thin strips. Combine lamb and rind in large bowl, pour over combined juice, garlic, rosemary, pepper, mustard and oil, mix well; cover, refrigerate overnight.
2 Preheat oven to moderate.
3 Drain lamb from marinade; reserve marinade. Thread lamb onto 16 skewers. Heat extra oil in baking dish, add kebabs in batches; cook, turning occasionally, until lightly browned.
4 Return kebabs to baking dish and pour over reserved marinade. Bake, uncovered, in moderate oven 15 minutes or until tender.
5 Remove kebabs from baking dish, boil marinade in dish, uncovered, until reduced to 1½ cups (375ml); add butter, stir until melted. Serve sauce with kebabs.

makes 16

lamb & haricot bean casserole

2 cups (400g) dried haricot beans
2kg leg of lamb, butterflied
¼ cup (60ml) olive oil
2 medium onions, chopped
2 cloves garlic, crushed
2 x 425g cans tomatoes
¼ cup (60ml) tomato paste
½ cup (125ml) dry red wine
1 cinnamon stick
1 tablespoon lemon juice
2 tablespoons chopped fresh parsley

1 Place beans in bowl, cover well with cold water; cover, stand overnight. Drain beans, add to saucepan of boiling water, simmer, uncovered, 30 minutes or until tender; drain well.
2 Cut lamb into 3cm pieces. Heat oil in saucepan, cook lamb, in batches, until well browned; remove from pan. Add onions and garlic to same pan, cook, stirring, until onions are soft; return lamb to pan.
3 Stir in undrained crushed tomatoes, paste, wine and cinnamon; simmer, covered, 2 hours or until lamb is tender, stirring occasionally.
4 Add beans, juice and parsley to pan; season with salt and pepper to taste, stir over heat until heated through. Discard cinnamon stick before serving.

serves 6

lamb & green bean casserole

1 tablespoon olive oil
500g diced lamb
1 large onion (200g), chopped
   finely
1 teaspoon ground coriander
½ teaspoon ground allspice
½ teaspoon cracked black pepper
400g can tomatoes
2 tablespoons tomato paste
1 cup (250ml) chicken stock
350g baby green beans, trimmed
2 cloves garlic, crushed
2 tablespoons finely chopped
   fresh flat-leaf parsley

1 Heat oil in 2-litre (8-cup) deep flameproof dish; cook lamb, in batches, until browned. Return lamb to dish with onion and spices; cook, stirring, until onion is soft. Add undrained crushed tomatoes, paste and stock; bring to a boil.
2 Bake, covered, in moderate oven about 1½ hours or until lamb is tender. Stir in beans; bake, uncovered, a further 5 minutes or until beans are just tender.
3 Just before serving, stir in garlic; sprinkle with parsley.

serves 4

lamb roasts with citrus tabbouleh

2 tablespoons sumac
2 tablespoons olive oil
1 clove garlic, crushed
4 mini lamb roasts (800g)
200ml plain yogurt
citrus tabbouleh
½ cup (80g) bulgar wheat
1 cup coarsely chopped fresh
    flat-leaf parsley
6 small tomatoes (780g), deseeded,
    chopped finely
2 tablespoons coarsely chopped
    fresh mint leaves
2 tablespoons finely grated
    lemon rind
2 tablespoons lemon juice
2 cloves garlic, crushed
1 teaspoon cracked black pepper

1 Combine sumac, oil and garlic in large shallow dish, add lamb; mix well. Cover; refrigerate 3 hours or overnight.
2 Cook lamb, uncovered, on heated oiled barbecue (or grill or char-grill) until browned all over and cooked as desired.
3 Serve lamb with yogurt and citrus tabbouleh.

citrus tabbouleh Place bulgar wheat in small bowl, cover with cold water, stand 15 minutes; drain. Rinse bulgar wheat under cold water, drain; squeeze to remove excess moisture. Combine bulgar wheat in medium bowl with remaining ingredients.

serves 4

37

lamb, aubergine & prune tagine

2 medium (600g) aubergines
coarse cooking salt
¼ cup (60ml) olive oil
1kg diced lamb
½ teaspoon ground cinnamon
2 teaspoons ground cumin
½ teaspoon ground ginger
1 teaspoon ground turmeric
2 cloves garlic, crushed
1 large (200g) onion, finely chopped
2¾ cups (680ml) water
2 strips lemon rind
1 cinnamon stick
¾ cup (125g) pitted prunes, halved
½ cup (80g) blanched almonds, toasted
1 tablespoon honey
2 tablespoons chopped fresh coriander leaves
2 teaspoons sesame seeds, toasted

1 Cut aubergines into 1cm slices, place in colander, sprinkle with salt; stand 30 minutes. Rinse slices under cold water, drain, cut into quarters.
2 Heat oil in pan, add lamb and ground spices, cook, stirring, until lamb is browned all over; remove from pan. Add garlic and onion to pan, cook, stirring, until onion is soft. Stir in water, rind and cinnamon stick. Return lamb to pan, simmer, covered, about 1 hour or until lamb is just tender.
3 Stir in prunes, nuts, honey, coriander and aubergines, simmer, covered, 30 minutes or until aubergines are tender. Discard cinnamon stick and rind.
4 Serve tagine sprinkled with sesame seeds.

serves 6

braised lamb & aubergine with pilaf

1 large aubergine (500g)
coarse cooking salt
2 tablespoons olive oil
1 large red onion (300g), finely chopped
3 cloves garlic, crushed
600g chopped lean lamb
½ teaspoon ground cinnamon
¼ teaspoon ground cardamom
½ teaspoon garam masala
1 teaspoon ground cumin
2 cups (500ml) water
2 cups (400g) basmati rice
3 cups (750ml) chicken stock
1 cup (150g) unsalted roasted cashews
5 medium tomatoes (600g), peeled, deseeded, chopped
¼ cup chopped fresh coriander leaves

1 Cut aubergine into 1cm slices, place in colander, sprinkle with salt, stand 30 minutes. Rinse aubergine slices under cold water, drain on absorbent paper; chop aubergine.

2 Heat half the oil in large pan, add onion and garlic, cook, stirring, until onion is soft; remove from pan.

3 Cut lamb into 2cm pieces. Heat remaining oil in same pan, add lamb, cook until browned all over, add spices, cook, stirring, until fragrant. Add onion mixture and water, simmer, covered, 45 minutes, stirring occasionally.

4 Add aubergine, simmer, covered, 45 minutes or until aubergine and lamb are tender.

5 Meanwhile, place rice in bowl, cover with hot water, stand until cool, rinse under cold water; drain.

6 Add stock to large heavy-based pan, bring to boil, add rice, simmer, covered with tight-fitting lid, 12 minutes. Remove from heat, stand 10 minutes. Stir in nuts, tomatoes and coriander. Serve pilaf topped with lamb and aubergine mixture.

serves 4 to 6

spicy lamb racks with quince

6 medium quinces (2kg)
2 tablespoons olive oil
60g butter
1 clove garlic, crushed
1 teaspoon ground cumin
1 teaspoon coriander seeds, crushed
⅔ cup (160ml) dry white wine
¼ cup (50g) brown sugar
spicy lamb racks
2 tablespoons olive oil
1 tablespoon honey
2 teaspoons ground cumin
1½ teaspoons ground coriander
1 teaspoon ground turmeric
½ teaspoon ground allspice
¼ teaspoon cayenne pepper
6 racks (1kg) lamb (3 cutlets each)

1 Peel quinces, cut each quince into eight pieces; remove cores.
2 Heat oil, butter, garlic and spices in large baking dish, cook, stirring, until fragrant. Add quinces, cook, stirring, about 5 minutes or until lightly browned. Stir in wine and sugar. Bake, uncovered, in moderate oven about 45 minutes or until quinces are pale pink and lightly browned, stirring occasionally.
3 Place spicy lamb racks on top of quinces in baking dish. Bake, uncovered, in moderate oven about 15 minutes or until lamb is tender.

spicy lamb racks Combine 1 tablespoon of the oil with honey and spices in bowl; mix well. Brush lamb with spice mixture, cover; refrigerate several hours or overnight. Heat remaining oil in pan, add lamb in batches, cook until browned all over.

serves 6

lebanese-style lamb pizzas

2 tablespoons olive oil
1 medium (150g) onion, chopped finely
1 clove garlic, crushed
500g minced lamb
¼ teaspoon cayenne pepper
2 teaspoons ground cumin
½ teaspoon ground cinnamon
1 cup (250ml) beef stock
2 medium (280g) tomatoes, chopped finely
⅓ cup (50g) pine nuts, toasted
¼ cup coarsely chopped fresh flat-leaf parsley
⅓ cup coarsely chopped fresh mint
4 individual pizza bases
280g jar char-grilled aubergine, drained
1 cup (280g) natural yogurt
1 teaspoon sumac

1 Preheat the oven to hot.
2 Heat oil in a large frying pan; add onion and garlic, cook, stirring, until onion is soft. Add mince; cook, stirring, until browned. Add pepper and spices; stir until fragrant.
3 Add stock and tomatoes to the pan and cook, stirring, over a medium heat until most of the liquid is evaporated. Remove from the heat, stir in the pine nuts, parsley and half the mint.
4 Place pizza bases on greased baking trays. Top each pizza base with aubergine, then press mince mixture onto aubergine, leaving a 3cm border.
5 Bake on lower shelf in a hot oven for about 12 minutes or until browned lightly.
6 Serve the pizzas topped with yogurt and sprinkled with the remaining mint and sumac.

serves 4
tip Sumac is a Middle Eastern spice with a tangy flavour, available from major supermarkets.

aubergines with pumpkin & feta

4 medium aubergines (1.2kg),
  halved
coarse cooking salt
¼ cup (60ml) olive oil
200g piece pumpkin, finely
  chopped
1 small onion (80g), finely chopped
2 cloves garlic, crushed
1 teaspoon ground cumin
2 tablespoons brown sugar
1 cup cooked long-grain rice
2 tablespoons chopped fresh
  coriander leaves
⅓ cup (50g) hazelnuts, toasted,
  chopped
100g feta cheese, crumbled

1 Sprinkle cut surface of aubergines with salt, place on wire rack over dish, stand 30 minutes. Rinse aubergines, pat dry with absorbent paper. Brush cut surface of aubergines with half the oil, place on wire rack over baking dish. Bake, uncovered, in moderate oven about 40 minutes or until aubergines are tender; cool 10 minutes.

2 Scoop flesh from aubergines, leaving 5mm shells. Chop aubergine flesh.

3 Heat remaining oil in pan, add pumpkin, onion, garlic and cumin; cook, stirring, until pumpkin is just tender. Stir in aubergine flesh, sugar, rice, coriander and nuts.

4 Divide pumpkin mixture among aubergine shells, place on oven tray; top with cheese. Bake in moderate oven about 30 minutes or until cheese is lightly browned.

serves 4
tip You will need to cook ⅓ cup (65g) rice for this recipe.

fattoush

2 large pitta breads
2 tablespoons olive oil
1 clove garlic, crushed
2 small cucumbers (260g), thinly sliced
4 medium plum tomatoes (300g), quartered
1 medium red pepper (200g), chopped
6 spring onions, chopped
2 tablespoons chopped fresh parsley
1 tablespoon chopped fresh mint
dressing
⅓ cup (80ml) lemon juice
¼ cup (60ml) light olive oil
1 clove garlic, crushed
1 teaspoon ground sweet paprika
¼ teaspoon ground cumin
¼ teaspoon freshly ground black pepper

1 Brush each side of pitta bread with combined oil and garlic, place bread on baking tray. Toast in moderately hot oven about 15 minutes or until crisp; cool. Break bread into bite-size pieces.
2 Combine cucumbers, tomatoes, pepper, onions and herbs in bowl.
3 Just before serving, add bread; drizzle fattoush with dressing.

dressing Place all ingredients in jar; shake well.

serves 4

artichoke & vegetable salad

3 large carrots (540g)
⅓ cup (80ml) virgin olive oil
1 medium onion (150g), finely chopped
1 teaspoon coriander seeds, crushed
2 teaspoons chopped fresh thyme
4 medium potatoes (800g), quartered
½ cup (125ml) dry white wine
1 cup (250ml) water
½ medium cos lettuce, chopped
400g can artichoke hearts in brine, drained, quartered
1 tablespoon lemon juice
1 teaspoon cracked black pepper

1 Cut carrots in half, then in half again lengthways.
2 Heat 1 tablespoon of the oil in pan, add onion, coriander and thyme, cook, stirring, until onion is soft.
3 Add carrots and potatoes to pan, cook, stirring, 5 minutes. Add remaining oil, wine and water, simmer, covered, about 10 minutes or until just tender. Stir in remaining ingredients.

serves 4 to 6

beans with walnut tomato sauce

1kg green beans
425g can tomatoes
1 tablespoon olive oil
2 cloves garlic, crushed
2 teaspoons ground cumin
2 teaspoons ground coriander
¼ teaspoon cayenne pepper
¾ cup (90g) chopped walnuts, toasted
½ cup chopped coriander leaves
1 teaspoon sugar
1 small red pepper (150g), thinly sliced
1 small yellow pepper (150g), thinly sliced

1 Boil, steam or microwave beans until tender; drain.
2 Blend or process undrained tomatoes until smooth.
3 Heat oil in pan, add garlic, ground spices and nuts, cook, stirring, until fragrant. Add tomatoes, fresh coriander and sugar, cook, stirring, until heated through. Remove from heat, stir in pepper.
4 Combine beans with pepper mixture in large bowl; mix well.

serves 6 to 8

tabbouleh

⅔ cup (110g) bulgar wheat
6 cups firmly packed fresh flat-leaf parsley, coarsely chopped
½ cup coarsely chopped fresh mint
5 large tomatoes (1.25kg), finely chopped
2 medium onions (300g), finely chopped
2 spring onions, finely chopped
¾ cup (180ml) olive oil
¾ cup (180ml) lemon juice

1 Cover bulgar wheat with cold water, stand 15 minutes. Drain, press as much water as possible from bulgar wheat. Place bulgar wheat in large bowl.
2 Add remaining ingredients to bowl, mix gently until combined.

serves 6 to 8

spicy vegetables with chickpeas

2 large aubergines (1kg)
coarse cooking salt
⅓ cup (80ml) olive oil
1 medium leek (350g), chopped
2 cloves garlic, crushed
1 teaspoon ground cumin
1 teaspoon ground cardamom
1 teaspoon ground turmeric
1 teaspoon ground sweet paprika
½ teaspoon ground cinnamon
2 x 425g cans tomatoes
425g can chickpeas, rinsed,
    drained
3 small courgettes (270g), sliced
150g green beans, halved
350g baby yellow squash, halved
200g baby carrots, halved
½ cup (75g) pistachios, toasted,
    chopped
⅓ cup chopped fresh parsley
¼ cup chopped fresh mint
¼ cup chopped fresh coriander
    leaves
1½ cups (375ml) vegetable stock
500g spinach, shredded

1 Cut aubergines into 1cm slices, place in colander, sprinkle with salt, stand 30 minutes. Rinse slices under cold water, drain, pat dry with absorbent paper. Brush slices with half the oil, place in single layer on oven trays, grill on both sides until lightly browned; drain on absorbent paper. Cut slices in half.

2 Heat remaining oil in pan, add leek, garlic and spices, cook, stirring, until leek is soft. Add undrained crushed tomatoes, chickpeas, vegetables, nuts, herbs and stock, simmer, covered, until vegetables are tender.

3 Add spinach and aubergines to vegetable mixture, simmer, covered, about 5 minutes or until spinach is wilted.

serves 6

megadarra

1 cup (200g) brown lentils
2½ cups (625ml) water
½ cup (100g) white long-grain rice
3 cups (750ml) water, extra
1 teaspoon ground allspice
1 teaspoon ground coriander
1 teaspoon salt
1 teaspoon freshly ground black pepper
caramelised onions
¼ cup (60ml) olive oil
3 large onions (600g), halved, sliced
3 teaspoons sugar
1 tablespoon balsamic vinegar
½ cup (125ml) water

1 Combine lentils and water in medium pan, simmer, covered, about 25 minutes or until just tender.
2 Add rice, extra water, spices, salt, pepper and half the caramelised onions, cook, stirring, until mixture boils. Simmer, covered, stirring occasionally, about 15 minutes or until rice is tender.
3 Serve megadarra warm or cold, topped with remaining caramelised onions.

caramelised onions Heat oil in pan, add onions and sugar, cook, stirring, 5 minutes. Add vinegar and half the water, cook, stirring, about 10 minutes. Add remaining water, cook about 5 minutes or until onions are caramelised.

serves 4

grilled vegetable & haloumi wraps

3 baby (180g) aubergines, sliced thinly
2 medium (240g) courgettes, sliced thinly
1 small (250g) sweet potato, sliced thinly
1 medium (200g) red pepper, sliced thickly
1 medium (200g) yellow pepper, sliced thickly
2 tablespoons olive oil
1 teaspoon dried oregano leaves
salt and freshly ground black pepper
⅓ cup (80ml) lemon juice
3 cloves garlic, crushed
4 large pitta breads
¾ cup (200g) plain yogurt
1 teaspoon sweet paprika
250g haloumi cheese, sliced
75g baby spinach leaves

1 Heat a barbecue (or grill pan or non-stick frying pan).
2 Combine aubergine, courgettes, sweet potatoes, peppers, oil, oregano, salt, pepper, half the juice and half the garlic in a large bowl.
3 Cook vegetables on a heated barbecue (or grill pan or frying pan), in batches, until tender. Transfer to a serving platter; cover to keep warm. Add pitta bread to barbecue, cook until browned lightly on both sides and just heated through.
4 Combine remaining juice and garlic with yogurt and paprika in a small bowl.
5 Barbecue haloumi until browned on both sides and heated through.
6 Divide vegetables and haloumi among warm pitta breads; top with baby spinach. Drizzle with yogurt mixture and wrap tightly to enclose filling.

serves 4

tip Haloumi is a salty cheese originating in Cyprus. When fried or barbecued over a high heat, the outside becomes crisp, while the inside melts. It's best eaten straight away, as it becomes rubbery on cooling.

chickpeas with spinach & spices

2 tablespoons olive oil
1 medium onion (150g), chopped
3 cloves garlic, crushed
1 teaspoon ground cinnamon
1 teaspoon ground sweet paprika
2 teaspoons ground coriander
2 teaspoons cumin seeds
3 x 425g cans chickpeas, rinsed, drained
3 small tomatoes (300g), chopped
2 tablespoons tomato paste
¼ cup (40g) stoned chopped dates
1 cup (250ml) water
¼ cup chopped fresh coriander leaves
2 tablespoons chopped fresh mint
500g spinach, chopped

1 Heat oil in pan, add onion, garlic and spices, cook, stirring, until onion is soft.
2 Stir in chickpeas, tomatoes, paste and dates; then stir in water and herbs, simmer, covered, about 10 minutes.
3 Stir in spinach, simmer, uncovered, about 5 minutes or until spinach is just wilted.

serves 4 to 6

glossary

allspice also known as pimento or jamaican pepper; available whole or ground.

almonds

blanched skins removed.

slivered cut lengthways.

artichoke hearts tender centre of the globe artichoke; purchased in brine canned or in jars.

aubergines also known as eggplant. Depending on their age, they may need to be sliced and salted to reduce their bitterness. Rinse and dry well before use.

balsamic vinegar made from a regional wine of white trebbiano grapes specially processed then aged in antique wooden casks to give it a pungent flavour.

beans

green also called french beans.

haricot small, white, oval beans with a smooth texture and bland in flavour. Require soaking.

bulgar wheat also known as burghul; hulled steamed wheat kernels that, once dried, are crushed into various size grains.

caraway seeds a member of the parsley family; available in seed or ground form.

cayenne pepper thin-fleshed, long, very-hot red chilli; usually purchased dried and ground.

cheese

feta a crumbly textured goat's- or sheep's-milk cheese with a sharp, salty taste.

haloumi a firm, cream-coloured sheep's milk cheese matured in brine; can be grilled or fried, briefly, without breaking down.

chickpeas also called garbanzos, hummus or channa; an irregularly round, sandy-coloured legume.

chilli powder the Asian variety is the hottest, made from ground chillies; it can be used as a substitute for fresh

chillies in the proportion of ½ teaspoon ground chilli powder to 1 medium chopped fresh chilli.

cinnamon stick dried inner bark of the shoots of the cinnamon tree.

coriander also known as cilantro and Chinese parsley. A strongly flavoured herb, available fresh, ground and in seed form.

cornflour also known as cornstarch; used as a thickening agent in cooking.

courgettes also known as zucchini.

couscous a fine, grain-like cereal product, made from semolina.

cumin available both ground and as whole seeds; cumin has a warm, earthy, rather strong flavour.

flat-leaf parsley also known as continental parsley or italian parsley.

garam masala a blend of spices based on varying proportions of cardamom, cinnamon, cloves, coriander, fennel and cumin, roasted and ground together. Black pepper and chilli can be added for a hotter version.

ghee clarified butter; with the milk solids removed, this fat can be heated to a very high temperature without burning.

ginger also known as green or root ginger; the thick gnarled root of a tropical plant.

herbs we have specified when to use fresh or dried herbs. Use dried (not ground) herbs in the proportions of 1:4 for fresh herbs, for example 1 teaspoon dried herbs instead of 4 teaspoons (1 tablespoon) chopped fresh herbs.

lavash flat sheets of unleavened bread.

lentils varieties of dried legumes, identified by and named after their colour.

nutmeg available whole or in ground form.

olive oil mono-unsaturated; made from pressing tree-ripened olives. Extra virgin and virgin are the best,

obtained from the first pressings of the olive, while extra light or light refers to the taste, not fat levels.

paprika ground dried red pepper; available sweet or hot.

pine nuts also known as pignoli; small, cream-coloured kernels obtained from the cones of different varieties of pine trees.

pistachios pale green, delicately flavoured nut inside hard off-white shells. To peel, soak shelled nuts in boiling water about 5 minutes; drain, then pat dry.

pitta bread a slightly leavened, soft, flat bread. When baked, the bread puffs up, leaving a hollow, like a pocket, which can then be stuffed with savoury fillings.

quince yellow-skinned fruit with hard texture and acid taste.

rice

basmati fragrant, long-grained white rice. Wash several times before cooking.

calrose a medium-grain rice that is extremely versatile; you can substitute short- or long-grain rice if necessary.

long-grain elongated grain, remains separate when cooked; most popular steaming rice in Asia.

sesame seeds black and white are the most common of these tiny oval seeds; a good source of calcium.

sumac a deep-purple-red astringent spice coarsely ground from berries growing on wild Mediterranean shrubs, sumac adds a tart, lemony flavour to dips and dressings. Available from Middle Eastern food stores and specialty spice stores.

tagine a round dish with a conical lid; also name of a recipe for meat or vegetable stew with fruit and nuts.

turmeric a member of the ginger family, its root is dried and ground; pungent in taste but not hot.

yeast allow 2 teaspoons (7g) dried yeast to each 15g compressed yeast if substituting.

conversion charts

MEASURES

The cup and spoon measurements used in this book are metric: one measuring cup holds approximately 250ml; one metric tablespoon holds 20ml; one metric teaspoon holds 5ml.

All cup and spoon measurements are level.

The most accurate way of measuring dry ingredients is to weigh them. When measuring liquids, use a clear glass or plastic jug with metric markings.

We use large eggs with an average weight of 60g.

warning This book may contain recipes for dishes made with raw or lightly cooked eggs. These should be avoided by vulnerable people such as pregnant and nursing mothers, invalids, the elderly, babies and young children.

DRY MEASURES

METRIC	IMPERIAL
15g	½oz
30g	1oz
60g	2oz
90g	3oz
125g	4oz (¼lb)
155g	5oz
185g	6oz
220g	7oz
250g	8oz (½lb)
280g	9oz
315g	10oz
345g	11oz
375g	12oz (¾lb)
410g	13oz
440g	14oz
470g	15oz
500g	16oz (1lb)
750g	24oz (1½lb)
1kg	32oz (2lb)

LIQUID MEASURES

METRIC	IMPERIAL
30ml	1 fl oz
60ml	2 fl oz
100ml	3 fl oz
125ml	4 fl oz
150ml	5 fl oz (¼ pint/1 gill)
190ml	6 fl oz
250ml	8 fl oz
300ml	10 fl oz (½ pint)
500ml	16 fl oz
600ml	20 fl oz (1 pint)
1000ml (1 litre)	1¾ pints

LENGTH MEASURES

METRIC	IMPERIAL
3mm	⅛in
6mm	¼in
1cm	½in
2cm	¾in
2.5cm	1in
5cm	2in
6cm	2½in
8cm	3in
10cm	4in
13cm	5in
15cm	6in
18cm	7in
20cm	8in
23cm	9in
25cm	10in
28cm	11in
30cm	12in (1ft)

OVEN TEMPERATURES

These oven temperatures are only a guide for conventional ovens. For fan-assisted ovens, check the manufacturer's manual.

	°C (CELSIUS)	°F (FAHRENHEIT)	GAS MARK
Very low	120	250	½
Low	150	275–300	1–2
Moderately low	160	325	3
Moderate	180	350–375	4–5
Moderately hot	200	400	6
Hot	220	425–450	7–8
Very hot	240	475	9

index

A

apricots
chicken pilaf with apricots 30
chicken with apricots & cracked
wheat 22
artichoke & vegetable salad 51
aubergines
aubergines with pumpkin &
feta 47
lamb, aubergine & prune
tagine 38

B

barbecued chicken with lemon
& garlic 21
beans
beans with walnut tomato
sauce 52
lamb & green bean casserole 35
lamb & haricot bean casserole 34
braised chicken in tomato sauce
29
braised lamb & aubergine with
pilaf 41
bread
fattoush 48
grilled vegetable & haloumi
wraps 59
lavash bread 13
meatball soup with crispy pitta 6
bulgar wheat
kibbi 9
lamb roasts with citrus tabbouleh
37
lentil, bulgar wheat & spinach
soup 2
tabbouleh 53

C

cheese
aubergines with pumpkin & feta
47
grilled vegetable & haloumi
wraps 59
chicken
barbecued chicken with lemon
& garlic 21

braised chicken in tomato
sauce 29
chicken & rice soup 5
chicken kebabs with garlic
sauce 25
chicken pilaf with apricots 30
chicken tagine with dates &
honey 26
chicken with apricots & cracked
wheat 22
chicken with figs 18
roast chicken with rice stuffing 17
chickpeas
chickpeas with spinach &
spices 60
spicy vegetables with chickpeas
55
citrus tabbouleh 37
couscous 29
cracked wheat 22
crispy pitta 6
cucumber with minted yogurt 15

F

fattoush 48
figs, chicken with 18

G

garlic & lemon lamb kebabs 33
garlic sauce 25
grilled vegetable & haloumi wraps
59

K

kebabs
chicken kebabs with garlic
sauce 25
garlic & lemon lamb kebabs 33
lamb kofta 10
kibbi 9

L

lamb
braised lamb & aubergine with
pilaf 41
garlic & lemon lamb kebabs 33
kibbi 9

lamb & green bean casserole 35
lamb & haricot bean casserole 34
lamb kofta 10
lamb roasts with citrus tabbouleh
37
lamb, aubergine & prune tagine
38
lebanese-style lamb pizzas 44
meatball soup with crispy pitta 6
spicy lamb racks with quince 43
lavash bread 13
lebanese-style lamb pizzas 44
lemon
barbecued chicken with lemon
& garlic 21
garlic & lemon lamb kebabs 33
lentils
lentil, bulgar wheat & spinach
soup 2
megadarra 56

M

marinated olives 14
meatball soup with crispy pitta 6
megadarra 56

O

olives, marinated 14

P

pilaf
braised lamb & aubergine with
pilaf 41
chicken pilaf with apricots 30
pizzas, lebanese-style lamb 44
pumpkin & feta, aubergines with
47

Q

quince, spicy lamb racks with 43

R

rice
braised lamb & aubergine with
pilaf 41
chicken & rice soup 5
chicken pilaf with apricots 30